The situation
is under control

The situation
is under control

亜 真里男 | Mario A

ART DIVER

The situation is under control

亜 真里男［アーティスト］

私の、2013年の誕生日。
国際オリンピック委員会総会の演説で、我が国の安倍晋三内閣総理大臣が東京やフクシマについて「The situation is under control」と保証しました。はたして、その言葉を信じていいものでしょうか？
周知の通り、「3・11」関連のニュースは絶えることなく今日も続き、東日本大震災の悲しみは深く我々の心に残っています。私はこの経験を一生忘れることができないでしょう。日本のアーティストは、これを機に制作に対する姿勢を変え、作品構想をパラダイム・シフトさせ、大震災の問題に向き合っています。あの日以来、さまざまな立場からアーティストのステートメントが全国で発表され続けているのです。私にとっても、2011年から2016年に手掛けた作品は、これまでとこれからの長いキャリアの中で、特別な重みを持つ制作であると言えるでしょう。

今こそ、忌野清志郎をリーダーとした日本のロックバンド・RCサクセションが1988年にリリースした《サマータイム・ブルース》を、もう一度振り返り、愛聴しましょう。

> …あんたもこのごろ抜け毛が多い
> それでもTVは言っている「日本の原発は安全です」
> さっぱりわかんねえ、根拠がねえ
> これが最後のサマータイム・ブルース

この曲がリリースされた当時、私はドイツで「チェルノブイリ」の災害（の影響と脅威）を経験しました。
そして、2016年の現状。東京で暮らしてきた30年間……。

さて、東京オリンピック・パラリンピック組織委員会の試算によれば、2020年の大会運営に必要な費用が、当初見込みの3013億円から約6倍となる1兆8000億円に増大することが報道されました。
また、新国立競技場を巡っては、ザハ・ハディドのデザインが国際コンペの募集要項で1300億円程度とされた後、施工予定の建設会社から3000億円を超える見積もりが示されました。総理大臣が計画を白紙に戻して、ゼロベースで見直す事が、

まさに「The situation is NOT under control」を表していました。
Outstanding！

続いて争点にあげる象徴的なケースに、土地の評価額も含め総事業費1兆円を超える巨大プロジェクトがあります。三菱地所が建設する東京駅前の『日本一の超高層ビル』のことですが、私は都民の一人として強い疑問を抱きます。いわゆる「東京のグランドデザイン」の文脈で、土地価格を大幅に上回る状況に見えます。したがって、超高層ビルの建設から完成後のメンテナンスまで、膨大な金額・投資や電力が必要です。そしてそれらは、主に郊外の原子力発電に頼っているのです。この390メートルの高層ビルのための電力消費は、ほとんどが無駄で、人類や地球・環境に大きな損害を与えます。

三菱地所の杉山博孝社長が「世界の都市間競争が激しいといわれる中で、世界の人が『東京といえば常盤橋』と思い浮かぶような街にしたい」と述べたことに対して、偽装を感じます。むしろ、不動産開発の最近の状況は、日本のバブル期に起こったものと同じ社会構造と高級化スキームを思い出させます。

それまでの「東京の未来への哲学」は間違っていて、そこでは東京街づくりの担当者が家の建築構造や道路計画に対し、将来の環境を考えずに行動し、不動産関係者は利益しか考えておらず、地域住民の意見に耳を傾けません。

ある意味、社会契約説(social contract)を無視しています。社会が常に変化していく中で、意識的に、脱残業を実践している我々が、インターネットとフレックスタイムの時代に、はたして、何を求めているのでしょうか。

ファミリー・ライフのコンセプトに対する固定観念は、まだまだ進化の途上にあります。人間らしいワーク・ライフ・バランスの推進、子供の教育方法、かつての女性像・男性像がようやく解放され始めています。

私は、東京の非中央集権化を進めるために、人口、車、企業、庁舎を減らすと同時に、他の地域、県に移動させる都市計画が必要だと思っています。つまり、東京には、経済を動かすための新しい巨大な建築物や大手企業はもう必要ありません。それを理由に、原子力発電所が再稼動してしまうこの悪循環に気づいてください。

日本のアーティストとして、脱原発の国を実現させるためにできる限りのことをしたい。そのアート・プラクティスの一部として、国会前での反原発運動にも参加しました。2011年3月以降の状況を振り返れば、「フクシマから東京への風」の影響では、人口が密集する関東住民の避難が必須でしたが、国民は、それをどの程度認識していたでしょうか。この意識の低さは、選挙結果や投票率から分析できるとも言えます。

さて、私は、2016年でこの6年間制作してきた、東日本大震災に関する構造画を終

了します。以下がその作品群となります：

《Japan = Atom（ガイガー）、（フクシマ）、（天下り）*》(2011)
《ホットスポット》(2011)
《日本の海（I）、（II）》(2012)
《湾岸の家（I）、（II）、（未来）》(2012)
《When wrong attitudes become radioactive rice》(2013)
《Cool Japan》(2013)
《The situation is under control》(2014)
《Caroline in Hiroshima》(2014)
《イクメン》(2014)
《Ich liebe die japanische Kultur》(2014)
《when art is over》(2015)
《心》(2015)
《Love Me Tender》(2015)

また、「国際文化都市・東京」というスローガンや、2020年のオリンピックが目指す「世界が文化的魅力を感じる都市・東京」といったテーマを再確認し、あるいはそこに疑問を投じた、2016年の新しい油彩画を発表します：

《炉心溶融》*
《東京への風（ヒロシマ・ナガサキ・フクシマ）》
《原子力明るい未来のエネルギー》
《2012年8月17日、国会前「ATOMKRAFT？NEIN DANKE」（原子力？おことわり）》
独自のジャポニスム作風の《Gogh, Kiyoshiro & Me（Summertime Blues - Tokyo 2020）》。

日本美術史を巡る、亜 真里男の絵画とは何か。
これらの作品を一堂に集めた2016年の展示では、我が国日本、そして東京の美術文化の進化をご覧いただくことができるでしょう。さらに、鑑賞者の方々がこの作品をきっかけとして、多方面に行動を起こされることを願っています。創造性と魅力に満ちたこの東京において、私たちの生活がより社会的で優れたものとなるように、みなさんが多面的に考える時間を持ってくださることが、何よりの幸せです。

* 本書未収録

The situation is under control

Mario A [artist]

It was on my birthday in 2013.
At the International Olympic Committee, our Prime Minister Shinzo Abe guaranteed "the situation is under control" in regard to nuclear risks of Fukushima, Tokyo and other areas in Japan. But, how can we really believe it?
As you all know, we have been facing a constant stream of "3/11" related news continuing to thus today, and profound sorrow over the Great East Japan earthquake lies deep in our hearts. I will never forget this experience for the rest of my life.
Using various means, Japanese artists have been attempting to respond to issues exposed by the earthquake. Some have made alterations to their existing attitudes, and others have brought about paradigm shifts to what they were planning to create. Since that day, a wide variety of statements has been made public by our artists all over the country.
Considering my long career of artistic practice, I feel quite secure in declaring that my creations made from 2011 to 2016 can be perceived as highly significant, meaningful works of art.

Now, let's look back at "Summertime Blues" released in 1988 by RC Succession, a Japanese rock band led by Kiyoshiro Imawano, and listen to its lyric:

"...... Your hair's been thinning recently.
But TV says, 'Japanese nuclear power plants are safe!'
I can't understand it, there's no scientific fact.
This must be the last summertime blues".

In those days, I was in Germany and able to experience (the threat and consequences of) the Chernobyl catastrophe. Since then, now in 2016, 30 years of life in Tokyo have passed.

The Tokyo Organizing Committee of the Olympic and Paralympic Games has inflated the cost of Tokyo 2020 Olympic game to 1.8 trillion yen, almost six times greater than the initially stated 301.3 billion yen. The design competition of the New National Stadium required the construction cost to be around 130 billion yen, but the company that won its construction raised the estimate to over 300 million yen. Our Prime Minister jumped in the controversy to scrap the disputed deal, restarting another competition from scratch, which demonstrates how "the situation is NOT under control".
Outstanding!

Another symbolic case is a huge project to build a high-rise building whose total cost, including the estimated land price, exceeds 1 trillion yen. As a citizen of Tokyo, I feel strong doubt about this plan for "the highest skyscraper in Japan" in front of the Tokyo station. The project is contextualized in "Grand Design of Tokyo" while its prospect seems already far beyond the actual land value. Therefore, its construction and maintenance demand an overwhelming amount of money and investments, as well as electricity, which relies on nuclear power plants outside of Tokyo. However, power consumption for this 390 meter high landmark is mostly wasteful despite its negative influence to human well-being and the environment of our earth.

I sense something deceptive when Hirotaka Sugiyama, CEO of Mitsubishi Land Estate development, proclaims "In today's accelerating competitions among global cities, I want the name of Tokiwa-bashi (the name of the street on which the building is developed) to be the synonym of Tokyo for people all over the world". Rather, recent situations in real estate development remind me of the same social structures and gentrification schemes that took place during the disastrous "Japanese bubble era".

So-called "Tokyo's philosophy for the future" had many wrong issues, intolerable to a humanistic attitude towards work-life balance, especially regarding the emancipation of the Japanese woman, the emancipation of the Japanese man, child education and the concept of family-life.

Decision makers indifferent to long-term environmental consequences influence the structure of houses and road planning in Tokyo, and developers only pursue their profit without listening to local residents. It can be said that they neglect the idea of the social contract.

However, as we are living in a time of social mobility, we consciously work less overtime, what do we really want in this age of the internet and flextime?

To advance decentralization of Tokyo, I believe we need urban planning to help people, cars, corporations and ministry offices move to other regions outside of Tokyo.

In other words, Tokyo no longer needs gigantic buildings and huge corporations to boost a driving economy. We have to notice a vicious circle that lets nuclear power plants operate again in order to maintain those huge infrastructures in the megalopolis.

As an artist in Japan, I want to do whatever I can to help this country stop relying on the nuclear power. I joined anti-nuclear demonstrations in front of the diet building as part of my artistic practices.

Reflecting on situations after March, 2011, I wonder to what extent people of our nation were aware of the dangerous "wind blowing from Fukushima towards Tokyo", whose risks, if taken seriously, should have driven locals out of the highly-populated Kanto area to evacuate temporarily. The result of the latest elections and its voter turnout would help measure how low the risks were understood.

This year I will stop working on Japanese nuclear power issues in my "structural painting" series I have produced for the past six years. The body of works include:

"Japan = Atom (Geiger), (Fukushima), (Amakudari)* " (2011)
"Hotspot" (2011)
"Japanese Sea (I), (II)" (2012)
"Coastal House (I), (II), (Future)" (2012)

"When wrong attitudes become radioactive rice" (2013)
"Cool Japan" (2013)
"The situation is under control" (2014)
"Caroline in Hiroshima" (2014)
"Ikumen [Child-rearing Men]" (2014)
"Ich liebe die japanische Kultur" (2014)
"when art is over" (2015)
"Kokoro [Heart]" (2015)
"Love Me Tender" (2015)

Further, having in mind the slogan "Tokyo – Global Cultural City" and the theme "Tokyo as a culturally attractive city to the world" in the context of the Tokyo Olympics 2020, for the year 2016 the following oil paintings, either in an affirmative or doubtful way, will have been executed:

"Meltdown" *
"The Wind towards Tokyo (Hiroshima - Nagasaki - Fukushima)"
"Genshiryoku Akarui Mirai No Energy" (in English: "Nuclear Power, Energy For A Bright Future")
"2012. 8. 17, in front of the Parliament Building, "ATOMKRAFT? NEIN DANKE""
"Gogh, Kiyoshiro & Me (Summertime Blues - Tokyo 2020)" in a unique Japonism style.

In the context of Japanese art history, how should we examine Mario A's paintings? Visitors to this exhibition will see how our country's art culture in Tokyo has progressed. I also hope all of you visiting my exhibition will try taking action across diverse fields. I would really appreciate it if you could take your time for multi-layered consideration on possibilities of building a more humanistic society and better environments in our creative and charming Tokyo, to contribute to our nation's very lives.

* not included in this book

2 0 1 1

Japan = Atom（フクシマ）（部分）
Japan = Atom (Fukushima)
(Fukushima), detail

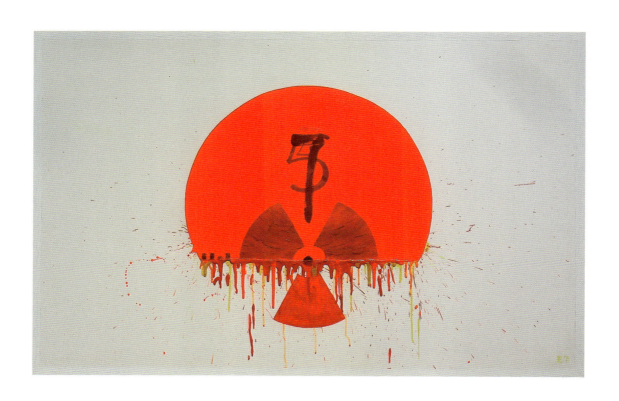

Japan = Atom (ガイガー) | *Japan = Atom (Gaiga)* (Geiger)

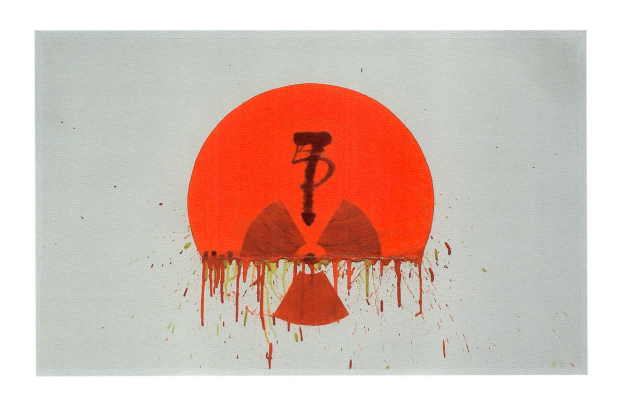

Japan = Atom (フクシマ) | *Japan = Atom (Fukushima)* (Fukushima)

ホットスポット
Hottosupotto (Hotspot)

2012

日本の海（I）| *Nihon no umi (I)* (Japanese Sea)

日本の海 (II) | *Nihon no umi* (II) (Japanese Sea)

湾岸の家(I)
Wangan no ie (I)
(Coastal House)

湾岸の家 (II) | *Wangan no ie (II)* (Coastal House)

湾岸の家(未来) | *Wangan no ie (Mirai)* (Coastal House / Future)

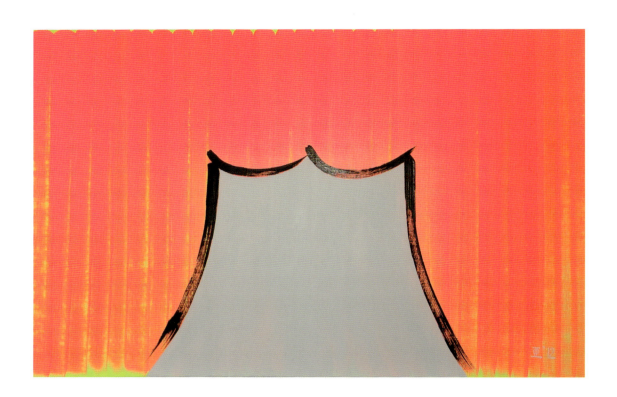

富士山(I) | *Fujisan (I)* (Mount Fuji)

富士山（大）| *Fujisan (Dai)* (Mount Fuji / Big)

2 0 1 3

Cool Japan（書、prototype A）| *Cool Japan* (Sho, Calligraphy, prototype A)

《Cool Japan（書、prototype A）》

「日展」が日本の美術を象徴するこの時代を、私たちはいつ脱することができるのでしょうか。身を以て模範を示すため、「クールジャパン」という、新たな「書」のシリーズを始めました。とはいえ、私は書家になる意思は、まったくありません。日本の書や美術に足りない表現を、「クールジャパン」の言葉のなかで、パラドキシカルに示すつもりです。
《Cool Japan（書、prototype A）》は、その結果としてできた最初のプロトタイプです。油彩画用のキャンバスに、墨ではなく「油」で「書」いています。
2013年9月18日のNHKニュースで、以下の報道がありました。

> 安倍総理大臣は、世界的な前衛芸術家の草間彌生さんと総理大臣官邸で面会し、政府が進めるクールジャパン戦略の一環として、日本の現代美術を世界に発信していきたいという考えを示しました。

このことがどういった意味を持つか、ぜひ考えていただきたい。
シリーズ「クールジャパン」は、単に我が国「日本」の現象を言葉でとらえるだけでなく、書を通して多義的な状況を表します。それは、読む側の潜在意識、あなたの精神の本質を見極めるものでもあるのです。つまり、「play the cool ... or not」。

東京、2013年12月13日
亜 真里男

《When wrong attitudes become radioactive rice》

鑑賞者に不快さや危機感を意識してもらうために新作をつくりました。《Cool Japan》と同様に、「bon mot」の文脈で、様々な制作方法と素材でイデアをインスタレーション化した作品であり、何にも勝る重要なアート・プラクティスです。

震災から2年半近くが経った今でも、仮設住宅問題は解決せず、「Atom Japan」を象徴する福島第一原発の汚染水が海洋に漏れ続けています。7月26日には放射性セシウムが、1リットル当たり23億5000万ベクレル検出されたとの発表がなされました。

国内だけではなく、世界の「仁義」にも非常に悪い態度(="wrong attitude")を示している日本政府と東京電力に、私たちは恥を知り耐えなければなりません。しかも、選挙結果から社会の精神虚弱の輪郭が見えてきました。7月21日の参院選投票率は52.6%、つまり、あなたの隣の人は現在の日本社会、経済、文化に対して無関心なのです。

ベネツィア・ビエンナーレやアートバーゼル、リステを訪問した際に、原発を完全に停止したスイス、イタリア、ドイツに立ち寄ると、「あなたの国、日本はどうなっていますか」と何度も聞かれました。私は、「憲法改正、国防軍への改組、ヒロシマ・ナガサキ・フクシマにもかかわらず、我が国にっぽんは原子力発電の再稼働や海外輸出をしている」という困った答えしかできませんでした。この「Uncool Japan」の中で、アーティストはどういう姿勢を示せばいいのでしょうか。

現状をよく見れば、外国の人に「日本の風潮は、反原発になっています」という答えも、最近は言えるようになりました。私のアンテナによると、日本の現代アート界では、アーティスト、キュレーター、ギャラリスト、コレクターのほとんどが反原発の立場をとっています。選挙結果からすると、我々はマイノリティです。しかし、具体的な行動（展覧会、デモ参加、アクティビストの発言）を通して強い影響力を持ち、この2年間、原発に対する日本国民のパラダイム・シフトを起こす力を示しています。

アフリカ系米国人のオバマの大統領選挙、ドイツの平和運動と「緑の党」の20年間の活動は、若い人にもいいヒントを与えてくれるでしょう。また、保守党のメルケル首相が原発を止めた原因は、ドイツの中流階級層の環境問題に対する認識が高まったからです。これらのことから、時間が経てば、次第に日本の中流階級層にも同じ認識を持たらし、当然、六ヶ所村の問題まで追求することになるでしょう。

《When wrong attitudes become radioactive rice》では、福島県産の米と木材、チェルノブイリと関連するロシア産ガイガー・カウンターを展示しています。木材は、2012年ベネツィア・ビエンナーレ国際建築展において、日本館（伊東豊雄コミッショナー、国際交流基金主催）がパヴィリオン賞（金獅子賞）を受賞した際、東日本大震災を隠喩する木の幹を展示し

When wrong attitudes become radioactive rice | *When wrong attitudes become radioactive rice*

たことに由来します。それらは、2013年のベネツィア・ビエンナーレで特別表彰に輝いた日本館でも展示され、「東日本大震災の経験を他者と共有することは可能か」と問う田中功起さんの企画展と関係しています。

また、インスタレーションを構成する1枚の写真。そこに写るのは、ART iTの元編集長小崎哲哉さんで、日本館前での突然の再会時に撮った記念写真です。よく見れば、リクリット・ティラバーニャのTシャツを着ています。そこには「ASIANS MUST EAT RICE」の文字。英語の「MUST」のニュアンスはさまざまです。例えば、「べき」ではなく「必要」の解釈もでき、それぞれの国の文化によって、受け取り方に違いがあります。「RICE」という言葉はTPP問題まで発展しますし、この「MUST EAT RICE」という言葉には深いテーマ性があります。かつて日本国民の一部はタイ米を捨てた時期がありましたが、タイ人のティラバーニャさんの言葉だからこそ、その事実を忘れるべきではないでしょう。「MUST」not forget。

もうひとつ重要なポイントは、ハラルド・ゼーマン(1933-2005)の存在です。1999年と2001年にベネツィア・ビエンナーレのアーティスティック・ディレクターを務めた彼の影響力を示した「Curating after Szeemann」という標語は今も胸に響いています。彼に敬意を払うため、私の作品名は「When attitudes become form」展(ベルン、1969年)を参考にしました。西洋、アジア(日本を含む)、その他世界のアートの歴史上、最も革命的で、次世代のキュレーターや、アーティストに強い影響を与えた「叙事企画展」でした。

東京、2013年8月6日
亜 真里男

When wrong attitudes become radioactive rice(部分) | *When wrong attitudes become radioactive rice (detail)*

2 0 1 4

Caroline in Hiroshima (Cool Japan) | *Caroline in Hiroshima* (Cool Japan)

《Caroline in Hiroshima(Cool Japan)》

ポストモダン・プラクティスとして、基本的に説明はしないのですが、今回の新作《Caroline in Hiroshima》に関しては、次のような状況説明が必要だと思っています。

我が国の選挙結果として、残念ながら、まもなく原発再稼働時代が始まります。海外に目を向ければ、尖閣諸島と中国、北朝鮮、ウクライナを侵略したロシアなど、それぞれに緊張が高まり、ヨーロッパやアジアの新冷戦、ポスト集団的防衛時代が始まったといえるでしょう。このことは、核兵器禁止条約の廃止に向けた流れを呼び込むことを推測させます。

国際的な核兵器禁止を目指しているオバマ大統領が、4月23日に来日します。来日は4度目(9歳時のものを含む)にもかかわらず、これまでの他の米国大統領と同じく、広島市と長崎市を一度も訪れたことはありません。

一方、キャロライン・ケネディは、叔父のエドワード・ケネディと共に1978年に初来日した際、広島市の原爆資料館を見学しています。さらに2013年12月には、駐日アメリカ合衆国大使として、被爆地の長崎市を訪問。原爆資料館を視察し「深く心を動かされた。可能な限り、被爆者の活動を支援していきたい」と所感を述べられました。

1982年、私が初めて日本に来て、参加したのが、広島平和記念式典と長崎原爆犠牲者慰霊平和祈念式典でした。その後、チェルノブイリやフクシマをリアルタイムに経験したことで人生行路は変わりました。

私は、「アメリカは核兵器を使用した唯一の核保有国として、行動を起こす道義的責任を有する」という発言をしたオバマ大統領に、この新作《Caroline in Hiroshima》を捧げます。

Mr. President, can you visit Hiroshima?
YES YOU CAN!

東京、2014年4月21日
亜 真里男

イクメン（Cool Japan）| *Ikumen* (Cool Japan / Child-rearing Men)

The situation is under control (Cool Japan) | *The situation is under control* (Cool Japan)

脱亜論 (Cool Japan) | *Datsu-a-ron* (Cool Japan / De-Asianization)

Ich liebe die japanische Kultur (Cool Japan) | *I love the Japanese Culture* (Cool Japan)

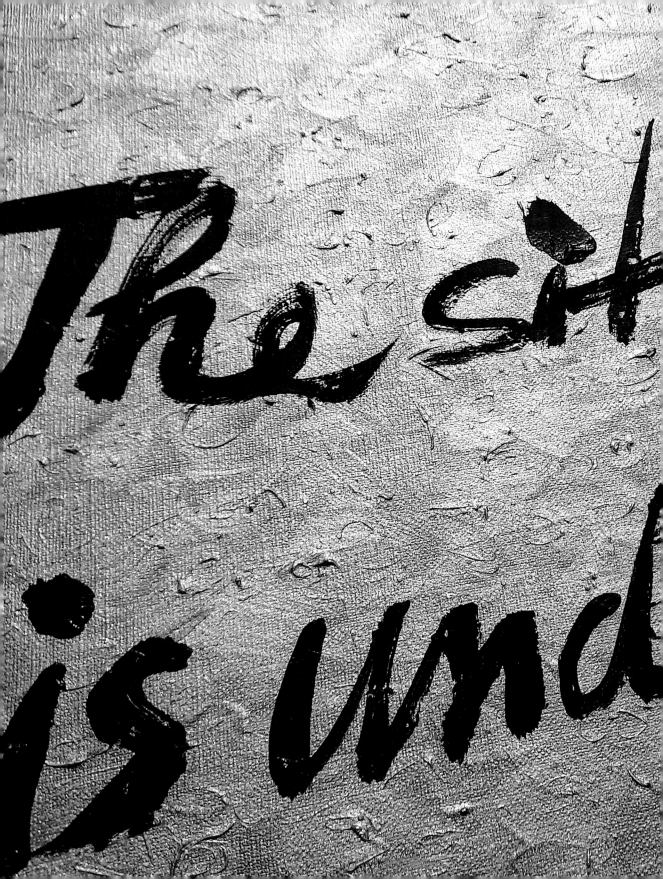

2 0 1 5

心(Cool Japan) | *Kokoro* (Cool Japan / Heart)

when art is over (Cool Japan) | *when art is over* (Cool Japan)

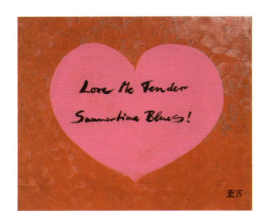

Beautiful Japan (Cool Japan)
Beautiful Japan (Cool Japan)

We ♡ Okinawa (Cool Japan)
We ♡ Okinawa (Cool Japan)

Love Me Tender (Cool Japan)
Love Me Tender (Cool Japan)

ricardian equivalence（Cool Japan）| *ricardian equivalence* (Cool Japan)

《Cool 九（Cool Japan）》

アート・プラクティスの一環として、8月30日、9月14日、9月16日、9月18日に国会周辺のデモに参加し、皆と一緒に大きな声で「憲法9条守れ！」などと「歌い」ました。そこに掲げたのが、《Cool Japan》シリーズとしての、毛筆のプラカード《Cool 九》です。

これまで、戦争体験に関する私の作品としては、自分の家族の戦争体験を綴ったシリーズ《ROBERTO》(＝ローマ・ベルリン・東京)、《ムッソリーニ》の彫刻(ミヅマアートギャラリー、2004)があります。当時のJapan Timesに載った、私の厳しい発言も参考になるでしょう。

2015年は戦後70年で、戦争関連の展覧会が各地で行われました。私は東京国立近代美術館「MOMATコレクション 特集：誰がためにたたかう？」に大変感動しました。テーマ展示「眼の戦争」では、Otto Dixを連想させる古沢岩美《餓鬼》(1952)、津田青楓《犠牲者》(1933)、《ブルジョア議会と民衆生活》下絵(1931)を見つけ、他セクションでは、我が国の現代アーティストの再認識もできました。戦争画のくくりは、納得する展示方法でした。

私は、日本のアーティストと違い、元ドイツ空軍人として拳銃、小銃、機関銃を使って人を殺す訓練を受けました。兵士の精神はヒエラルキーの文脈に従い「命令は絶対です」。殺さなければ敵に殺され、部下を命令する人間は狂信者です。同様に、嘘をつき間違ったイラク戦争を始めたブッシュ大統領と、2015年9月現在、大統領選挙の共和党指名候補争いでトップの支持率を保つドナルド・トランプ氏は共に、ルナティックの政治家です。トランプ氏の発言「Make America Great Again. America needs a victory again」は戦争準備に向けたパトリオットで大衆受けする選挙スローガンとなり、古い考えを持つ彼は冷戦を復活させる主戦論者です。もし、選挙の結果、トランプ氏が大統領になったら、どのようなきっかけで日米軍人が戦争に行くのでしょうか？

皆さまと一緒に「戦争を二度と繰り返さない」ことを願い、憧れの憲法9条(Cool 九)を、人類のために、現状のまま世界に広げることを願います。

第九条
一　日本国民は、正義と秩序を基調とする国際平和を誠実に希求し、国権の発動たる戦争と、武力による威嚇又は武力の行使は、国際紛争を解決する手段としては、永久にこれを放棄する。
二　前項の目的を達するため、陸海空軍その他の戦力は、これを保持しない。国の交戦権は、これを認めない。

東京、2015年9月5日＆9月29日
亜 真里男

Cool 九 (Cool Japan) | *Cool Kyu* (Cool Japan / Cool 9)

2 0 1 6

そうだ（オレンジ）｜ *Souda* (Soda / Orange)

そうだ（レモン）| *Souda* (Soda / Lemon)

H32（Cool Japan）| *H32* (Cool Japan)

美・サイレント(Cool Japan) | *Bi sairento* (Cool Japan / Be silent)
comme des garçons(Cool Japan) | *comme des garçons* (Cool Japan)

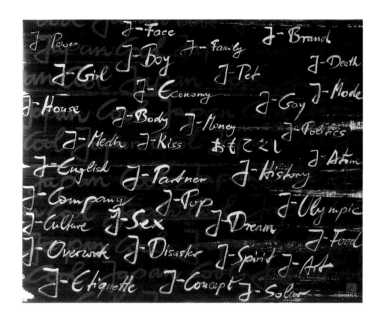

おもてなし（Cool Japan） | *O-mote-nashi* (Cool Japan / Japanese Hospitality)

Rauschenberg(Cool Japan) | *Rauschenberg* (Cool Japan)

東京への風（ヒロシマ・ナガサキ・フクシマ）（部分）
Toukyou he no kaze (hiroshima·nagasaki·fukushima) (The Wind towards Tokyo (Hiroshima – Nagasaki – Fukushima)), detail

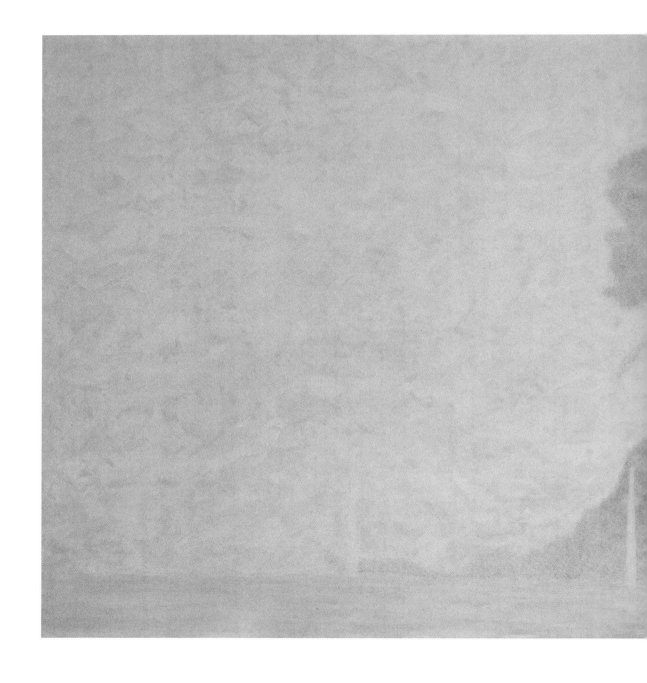

東京への風（ヒロシマ・ナガサキ・フクシマ）
Toukyou he no kaze (hiroshima・nagasaki・fukushima) (The Wind towards Tokyo (Hiroshima – Nagasaki – Fukushima))

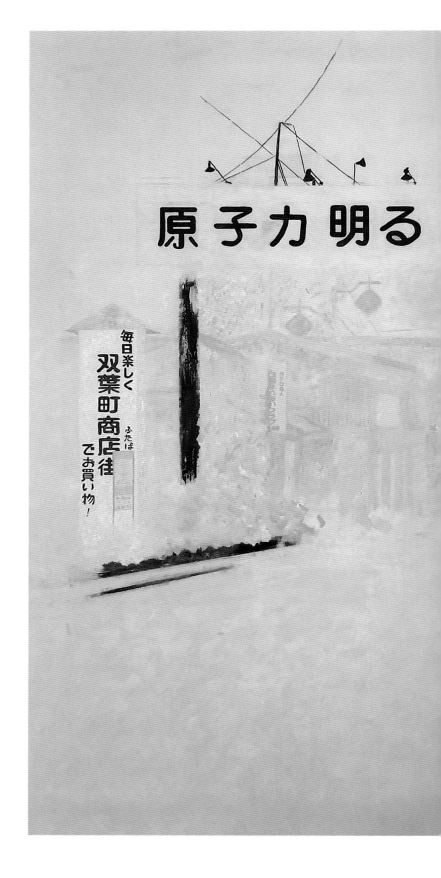

原子力明るい未来のエネルギー（未完）
Genshiryoku akarui mirai no enerugi
(Nuclear Power,
Energy for Bright Future)
(work in progress)

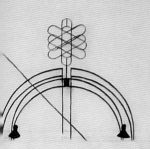

未来のエネルギー

《2012年8月17日、
国会前「ATOMKRAFT? NEIN DANKE」(原子力?おことわり)》

2012年8月、私は、毎週金曜日に首相官邸前で行われている反原発デモに参加していました。主催は首都圏反原発連合。その中心的存在であるミサオ・レッドウルフ氏とも知り合うことができました。

当初、デモは官邸前にて行われていましたが、引きが取れない場所のため、報道では官邸の建物とデモの参加者とが1枚の写真に収まらない。これではデモの規模が瞬時に伝わらないので、国会議事堂前をデモの中心としたらどうかと進言したこともありました。

やがてデモの中心は、官邸前から国会議事堂前に移りました。

そして8月17日の金曜日。私はいつものようにデモに参加しました。そこで目にしたのが、かつて見慣れた「ATOMKRAFT? NEIN DANKE」のシンボル。英語では、"Nuclear Power? No Thanks"、日本語だと「原子力? おことわり」、つまり反原発のシンボルです。これは、1970年代後半から80年代にかけてヨーロッパを中心に流行したもので、ステッカーを車やカバンに貼るなど、当時のドイツではあちらこちらで見かけたものでした。

今回のデモにおいては、アーティストの奈良美智さんが「NO NUKES」と記された自身の絵を自由に使っていいと、Twitterから呼びかけました。若者たちは奈良美智さんの絵をコンビニエンスストアでプリントアウトし、それをデモで掲げました。私はそのルーツに、「ATOMKRAFT? NEIN DANKE」を見たのです。

フクシマの事故を受けて、ドイツのメルケル首相は2022年までに原子力発電所を全廃することを決定しました。日本の原子力政策はどうなるのでしょうか。チェルノブイリとフクシマを経験し、東京で日本のアーティストとして活躍する私は、国会議事堂前に掲げられた「ATOMKRAFT? NEIN DANKE」の旗を、絵画として歴史に記録する意義を強く感じたのです。

2016年4月5日
亜 真里男

2012年8月17日、国会前
ATOMKRAFT? NEIN DANKE
（原子力？おことわり）（未完）
2012/8/17, Kokkai-mae
'ATOMKRAFT? NEIN DANKE'
(Genshiryoku? O-kotowari)
(2012.8.17, in front of
the Parlament building,
"ATOMKRAFT? NEIN DANKE")
(work in progress)

《Gogh, Kiyoshiro & Me (Summertime Blues - Tokyo 2020)》

私はジャポニスムが大好きです。日本語に翻訳すると「日本趣味」。ベルリン大学時代から、欧米における日本趣味の歴史や影響を国立図書館で調べ、今でもジャポニスム関係の本を集めています。ジャポニスムの「ズレ」「違和感」「妄想」「異国趣味」に強く惹かれます。自分のアーティスト活動の中には、「néo japonisme」(1996-)や「新日本画」(2008-)というシリーズがありますが、これらはジャポニスムの流れに位置する作品です。
日本美術史家・山下裕二氏の評論や、日本現代アーティストが自身の作品をジャポニスムと評するケースをしばしば見かけますが、それは間違った使い方です。定義上、ジャポニスムという専門用語は、「外国人が感じる日本趣味」であり、日本人が感じる日本趣味ではありません。
世界の絵画史では、クロード・モネ《ラ・ジャポネーズ》(1875-76)、ジェームズ・マクニール・ホイッスラー《La Princesse du Pay de la Porcelaine》(1863-1864)、ジョルジュ・ロシュグロス《Portrait de Sarah Bernhardt》(1900)、ジェームズ・ティソ《La Japonaise au bain》(1864年)などが、代表的な作品です。
はたして、《Gogh, Kiyoshiro & Me (Summertime Blues - Tokyo 2020)》は、ジャポニスムの歴史に名を残すことができるでしょうか。

2012年のアートフェア東京での個展にて、美術評論家・名古屋覚氏から、「あなたは日本で一番良い油絵画家です。そして、作品にイタリアのルーツを感じる」と言われました。考えてもいなかった言葉に、今後、より良い作品をつくることへの、将来への強いプレッシャーを感じました。キャンバスと格闘しながら、新しいジャポニスム(=和洋折衷)を生み出し、課題を解釈・解決し、いかに規則を曲げられるかに真剣に取り組む毎日です。
もう一つの楽しい試みは、鑑賞者や専門家に、様々なアートの遺伝子情報を解読(decode)させることです。今回は、好きなジャポニスム作品の一つである、ゴッホの《花魁》(1887)を再構築し、自分らしくゆがんだ画像に変形しました。そして《Summertime Blues》で2020年の東京オリンピックに向けたソーシャル・コメンタリーを発信し、「制御不能 = not under control」な現状に対して現れてきた変革の兆しを絵画化しています。東京オリンピックのポスターに選ばれることはないでしょうが……。
アートフェア東京2016で初公開される《Gogh, Kiyoshiro & Me (Summertime Blues - Tokyo 2020)》に込められた様々な隠喩と情報を楽しく解読してもらえれば幸いです。

東京、2016年3月22日
亜 真里男

Gogh, Kiyoshiro & Me
(Summertime Blues - Tokyo 2020)
Gogh, Kiyoshiro & Me
(Summertime Blues - Tokyo 2020)

Gogh, Kiyoshiro & Me

(Summertime Blues - Tokyo 2020)

Gogh, Kiyoshiro & Me

(Summertime Blues - Tokyo 2020)

ポスト情報化社会のアート —— 亜 真里男の場合

市原研太郎［美術評論家］

　一方で、至る所に情報が洪水となり、「情報の氾濫」という耳慣れたクリシェすら他の情報とぶつかり合って摩滅し、ほとんど無意味と化している。現今の過度な情報化社会は、しばしばこのようなものであると言われる。そのなかでアートは、どのようにすれば効果的な社会批判を投げかけ、目標の政治的変革を成し遂げられるだろうか？
　ところが他方で、情報が特定の狭い範囲に限定されて流通する。その際、「情報の氾濫」に貶下的な含意が付与されることで、情報の不平等な分配による「情報の貧困」の実態に蓋がされ、それに正当な判断を下すことができない状況が生まれる。アートは、情報に関するこの狡猾なイデオロギー的歪曲に、どう立ち向かうのか？
　アートの活動にとって不利な条件は、このような複雑な情報環境ばかりではない。未だに世間の先入見（高尚という美名の下での体の良い厄介払い）に悩まされている。この先入見もまた、情報をめぐる偏向（アートの情報が十全に供給されない）に由来するとすれば、アートが情報化社会で翻弄されている様子が、ありありと思い浮かぶのではないか。いずれにせよアートは、アートと情報にまつわる以上の現状認識に逆らって、アートの本来の使命を果たしていくことができるだろうか？
　とはいえ、中国などの非民主主義的な体制とは違って、インターネットやSNSが複雑に発達した日本の情報化社会では、誰でもメッセージ（意味のある情報）を発信することができる。だが、情報の氾濫は、情報に包囲され惑わされる人間に、記号とデータで作成された情報に対する不安と不信を呼び起こし、前述の情報の無意味化のみならず無価値化をもたらす。情報化社会で情報を扱うことを強いられるアートが、この困難を乗り越えて社会的、政治的に有効な表現を取り戻す方途はあるのだろうか？

　アートをめぐる以上の難問を一つひとつ解きほぐして、その原因に遡り解決策を練ることは容易なことではないが、情報化社会が、不平等や偏りがあるにせよ、総体的に見て情報の洪水に覆われていることは、これまでの記述で理解されるだろう。その結果として情報が無意味化したことは、すでに述べた。図式的に言えば、ある事柄に関してイエスとノーの両方の情報が、ほぼ同じくらい現実世界に溢れている。この条件では、それらの情報の真偽を確定することができない。それゆえ、肯定と否定の情報が衝突し、その意味が中和されて情報が無意味になる。この無意味な情報が、ノイズである。
　帰結が、情報が無意味となりノイズになることであれば、社会にさほど損害を与えないのではないか。社会は、そのような情報＝ノイズの発信を控えるよう、そしてそれを信じな

いように注意を払えばよい。あるいは、ノイズを純然たる無意味な記号に還元し、それを現実から切り離してアートの素材（情報の廃棄物）として利用することだってできる。ノイズは、自律的なアートにとっては格好の構成要素なのだ。

ところが、このノイズは、それを受け取る受信者の精神にダメージを与えないではおかない。情報に関して致命的になるかもしれない猜疑心を植え付けるのだ。無意味な情報は、とりもなおさず情報を発信しないことと同値である。これを言い直せば、発信された情報が無意味になるとは、それが意味作用しないことに等しいので、発信された記号は内容が欠落している。それが、受信者の精神に情報そのものに対する不信を惹き起こし、ついには一切の情報に価値がないとまで思い込ませる。情報が高度に発展した時代に伴って、人間の精神の内実である諸々の情報を腐蝕する悪しき副作用が、これである。こうした状況が出現するに至った時代を、ポスト情報化時代と呼んでおきたい。

とはいえ同時に、現実世界で分配される情報の格差が進行していて、有益な情報を持つ層と持たない層に分裂し、かつそのギャップが広がっている。それだけではない。情報を持つ者と持たない者との間で、経済的な格差が生じている。情報の多寡が、経済的な貧富の差につながるというわけだ。その事実を隠蔽するために、「情報の氾濫」といういい加減な標語がまことしやかに流布されていることは、すでに述べた通りである。だが、無意味化する「情報の氾濫」の裏面で、大量の情報の真偽を決定できず、どのように情報を処理したらよいか途方に暮れる人間（アーティスト）がいることを忘れてはならない。彼らは、情報の海に浮遊しながら、確たる地点に自らを投錨できず生きる実感を得られないでいるのである。一方で、情報世界を徐々に蝕む無意味化と無価値化の趨勢、他方で、権力を掌握するのに有用な情報を独占する階層の出現と、大量の情報に振り回され自己のアイデンティティを喪失した哀れな人間（アーティスト）。情報をめぐるこの両面的な現象は、直接・間接に情報を扱う現代アートに、無視できない深刻な影響を及ぼしている。それに対する反応としてまず想定されるのは、アートから極力情報を排除し、記号やデータではなく現物や実物を素材として用いるというものだ。そうでなければ反対に、現実に遍在する情報に呑み込まれるのではなく積極的に取り込み、効率的に管理・操作しながら表現をコントロールすることである。

日本では、この両極の他に選択の余地がないように見える。しかし、現物や実物を扱っていると思われる作品でさえ、情報化社会のなかでは少なからず情報に染め上げられていることは否定できない。どのような表現も情報に変換しなければ理解されない仕儀になっているのだ（昨今の作品に説明文が多いことに着目されたい）。だが、情報に対して依存も拒絶もしない例外的なやり方があるのではないか？　その例外を実践していると思われるアーティストの作品を取り上げて分析してみよう。そのアーティストの名前は、亜

真里男である。亜 真里男の2013年の作品に、《When wrong attitudes become radioactive rice》(32頁)がある。この作品は、いくつかのパートから成っている。その上部から順に、古い板に巻かれたカンヴァス、二人の人物が撮られた写真、張り出した丸棒に巻かれたカンヴァス、台座の上のロシア製ガイガーカウンター、そして下部の床に置かれた米袋である。これらのそれ自体ではとりたてて特徴のない素材＝部分の組み合わせは、相互に関係づけられることで緊迫した意味を帯びるようになる。

まず、そのなかの写真の中身を吟味することから取り掛かろう。被写体である前景の二人の人物の背後にある建物の壁につけられたネオンの文字と数字が重要である。「GIAPPONE 9478.57km」[1]。これは、記号とデータを組み合わせた情報であり、それを判読すれば、「日本まで9478.57km」となる。写真に写った建物、より特定して日本にある福島第一原発までその距離9478.57kmの場所とは、イタリアのヴェネツィアのビエンナーレ会場にある日本パビリオンのことだ。さらに、手前の右側の日本人らしき人物が着る白いTシャツにプリントされた英文は、「アジア人は米を食うべし」と訳される。この写真が、2011年3月11日の東日本大震災、とりわけ福島で勃発した原発事故に言及していることは明白だろう。

これまでの話の文脈で語れば、亜 真里男は、情報化社会で通常使用されている手段を動員して、作品の一部を構成していることは間違いない。とすれば、この作品が情報化社会のアートの例外であると主張できる証拠はまったくないように見える。だが、私が例外ということで言いたかったのは、情報を一切用いないということではない。否応なく押し寄せてくる情報に取り囲まれながらも、それによって仕掛けられた罠を、アートがいかにすり抜けるかということが重要なのである。

この作品は、情報のオーソドックスな使用を踏まえつつ、それを一瞬のうちに跨ぎ越して、直接対象（フクシマ）に到達する。作品の他の要素も、この狙いを強化するように注意深く選ばれ配置されている。アートのメタファーであるカンヴァスを巻いた板と棒の木材と、米袋に入った米は、福島から持って来られたものだ。それらの素材が浴びているかもしれない放射線を計るガイガーカウンターが、ケースの箱やマニュアルとともに置かれている。

以上の説明は、作品に直接印刷されているか、作品の横に付されたキャプションの情報から導いたものである。この作品は、情報を無理やり排除したり、逆に情報に全面的に依存し、情報の晦冥な海に溺れてその犠牲になることはない。それは、情報の包囲網を出し抜いて対象（深刻な原発事故）に到達する術を心得ているアーティストの絶妙なバランス感覚と冷静な取捨選択の賜物なのである。この感性と判断に、どのような普遍的な基準があるわけではない。その時々の状況に合わせて情報の包囲網を潜り抜け、鑑賞者をして目標に対面させるやり方を亜 真里男が心得ていることの証なのだ。

次に、亜 真里男の新作の絵画の説明に移ろう。彼が絵画という表現方法を採用したのは、彼が元々画家であることに主たる理由があるだろう。だがそれ以上に、絵画が現在陥っている絵画自身が気づかない窮状に、興味を抱いたことが重要な契機になっているのではないか？ すなわち、絵画の終焉が叫ばれて久しいにもかかわらず、絵画は生き延びているだけでなく、マーケットを中心に隆盛を維持している。この事態に、亜真里男は真正面からぶつかり、絵画は終わっていると無言で告知するのだ。と同時に、そのようなアートの逼迫した事情はお構いなしに、絵画を含めたアート全体を跨ぎ越して現実に働きかけるのである。それは、どのようにしてか？

絵画の死亡宣告は、過去に一度起きた。それは、1980年代のモダンの終わりに絵画の終焉が叫ばれたときである。それからすでに35年は経っているが、先述したように絵画は予言通り消滅するどころか、栄華を極めているように思われる。だが、優れた作品は少ない。というより、ほとんどないのではないか？ その理由は、現在絵画が本当に終わるのではないかという問いと密接に関連している。今度こそ終焉するのなら、優れた作品が少ないのは当然だろう。というのは、この時点で終わりを刻印する表現か、次の展開はひとまず措くとして、終わらせる表現以外に、興味を掻き立てる作品はないからである。では、なぜ絵画は終焉しつつあるのだろうか？ その推論は、ポストモダンの終わりの証明によって傍証されるだろう。なぜなら、絵画の終焉はポストモダンの終わりに付随した現象だからだ。ということは、ポストモダンの後の時代に、絵画は復活を遂げるかもしれないという予想が立つ。

ここで、ポストモダンが終わることの証明を試みてみよう。ここでポストモダンの原理を、簡潔に「シミュラークル」としておく。ポストモダンをこのように簡単に言い当てられないと考える向きには、モダンの原理は「物質」だったことを付け加えておこう。歴史を駆動する原理は実に単純だが、その成果やそこから派生する現象はすこぶる複雑なのである。

ところで「シミュラークル」とは、ボードリヤールによれば「モデルのないコピー」であり、その代表が「商品」だとされた。しかし、「商品」には指示対象となる設計図やモデルがあったので、厳密に言えば「商品」はシミュラークルではなくコピーだったのだ。このようにして、根源的に欠陥のあるアイデアから発想され開始されたポストモダンだったが、時代が下るにつれ、夾雑物（モデルの残滓）が混じる擬似的シミュラークルから、その夾雑物が取り除かれ純化されていった。少なくとも、アートとりわけ絵画は、その主戦場になったのである。

この歴史の端緒となったアーティストは、言うまでもなく1960年代に制作を開始したゲルハルト・リヒターである。彼の絵画の変遷は、シミュラークル（私の用語では「指示対象のないイメージ」）を具象と抽象の画面上で追求した個人史だったといって過言ではな

い。リヒターに後続する画家たちが、意識的、無意識的に彼の試みを受け入れ試行錯誤を重ねていったが、成功や失敗を繰り返しながら現在に至った。そのポストモダンの絵画の最終のゴールが、今はっきりと見えてきている。

そのゴールは、ポストモダンのパラダイムが消尽したことで、行く手を阻む障壁がなくなり現れてきた。その消尽を印す徴候は、二つある。一つは、アートがシミュラークルを生成するに当たり、引用の源が枯渇したことである。絵画が引用するのは、絵画の歴史である。そのリサイクルできる資源が、底をついた。過去に使用したものを再利用すること(リサイクルのリサイクル)はできるが、それをまともに実行しても当然前例が存在するので、シミュラークルにならずコピーにしかならない。それはポストモダンのゲームで、なんでもありのルールの唯一のあってはならない違反なのである。

次に、ポストモダンは引用した過去の諸要素をデフォルメするか組み合わせてシミュラークルを作成するのだが、その方法で生み出せるレパートリーがほぼ尽きてしまった。まだその可能性のメーターはゼロを指してはいないが、遅かれ早かれゼロになってシミュラークルは消滅し、あらゆるものが過去のコピーになるだろう。それによってポストモダンが終焉すると同時に歴史も終焉するなら、その刹那、歴史後の世界が訪れる。しかし、幸運にもそうならないとすれば、次世代の賢明な人類は、モダンでもポストモダンでもない新たな歴史の構築に乗り出すことだろう……。

さて、本題の亜 真里男の絵画を手短にまとめておこう。その肝は、彼が前述の絵画の終焉に対して鋭い自覚で制作に取り組んでいることである。ポストモダンの終焉の証拠となるのは、その構成要素の枯渇と方法の閉塞である。引用できる要素のアーカイヴが底をつき、その要素で作られるはずのシミュラークル絵画が霧散する。その現実を熟知した上で、彼が採用するやり方は、過去の歴史の全肯定である。具体的な活動としては、ポストモダンの時代と同じく、なにをやってもよい。だが、ポストモダンと決定的に違うところは、現代がなにをやってもなにかに似てしまう(これがポストモダンである)のではなく、まったく同一であると知っていることである。それによって、前掲の《When wrong attitudes become radioactive rice》と同様、一切の形式や方法を跨ぎ越し(もはや形式はないので内容もない)、直に対象に斬り込んでいく。彼の放つ批判の矢が、トートロジーと化した表現を打ち破って、対象の現実に突き刺さるのだ。

これが、情報化社会のあらゆる障害を乗り越えて、彼が批判する社会にピンポイントで介入する亜 真里男の鮮やかなマジックである。

1——このネオンは、2013年に開催された第55回ヴェネツィア・ビエンナーレの日本パビリオンに出展された田中功起さんの作品の一部です。

Art in the Age of Post-Information Society – the case of Mario A

Kentaro Ichihara [art critic]

On one hand, information overflows everywhere so that even a familiar cliche like "information overload" is worn out as a nonsense term in friction with other information. This is one of the typical ways we talk about today's information society. The question is how art, in such a saturated world, can effectively address critical visions on our social issues in order to make political reformations happen.
On the other, however, information is also circulated within selected small communities. In this context, the concept "information overload" connotes a somewhat derogatory attitude, unable to acknowledge and properly judge the reality of "info-poverty" resulting from unfair distribution of information. The question is, in turn, how art can confront this cunning ideological distortion revolving around information [politics].
In addition to such complex info-environments, artistic activities are facing further difficulties. Even today, art still suffers from a prejudice from the general public (that shun art as "highbrow" culture irrelevant to common people and not worthy of attention). If such predispositions are rooted in biased representations (that art is unfairly under-represented), it would be not hard to imagine art has lost its ground within tides of information society. In any case, it is debatable whether art today can achieve its primary objectives against [challenging] recognitions about art and information as mentioned above.
Having said this, the internet and SNS tools made available in highly advanced information society in Japan, unlike undemocratic ones like China, allow everyone to express any message (information with meanings). Yet, bewildered in the midst of too much information, people come to fear and distrust information provided in the form of sign and data, which deprives information of its meaning, as well as its value. Then, art in information society, which is bound to deal with information anyway, will ask a question – Can art overcome those challenges and recover expressive capabilities to influence our socio-political realities?

With all the difficulties facing art nowadays, it is not easy to disentangle those convoluted problems, one at a time, to probe their root causes and work out fundamental solutions, but it is at least possible to understand that information society at large is filled up with excessive information, even with inequalities and biases as I have so far described. I already pointed out how information has been turned into nonsense as a consequence. The real world, if outlined as a whole, can be seen as a flood of both positive and negative statements nearly in balance in regards to the subject matter. Under this circumstance one cannot judge the truthfulness of given information. Therefore, affirmation and negation contradict each other and neutralize them into nonsense. When information is nullified as such, it is called noise.
Some would imagine this causes no great harm to society as far as the consequence is just information becoming meaningless as noise. Then, they would suggest, society

should pay more attention to prevent us from making such information=noise and educate people not to believe it. Or, others would think noise can be used as a material for art (as information waste) by reducing it to purely meaningless signs fully separated from the reality. Art for art's sake may find noise as a favorable medium to constitute its autonomy.

However, noise is not harmless to the mind of its receivers. It will implant latent lethal skepticism about information. Sending nonsense information is equal to not signaling any message. In other words, a message becomes nonsense when it signifies nothing, meaning that the message lacks content. This invokes doubts about information in general, which will eventually lead to a misconception in that no information should have any meaning. In our highly advanced information society, we're suffering this side-effect that undermines the function of information as the essence of our mind. I would call this situation "the age of post-information society" for convenience of discussions to follow.

On the other hand, however, information has increasingly divided the real world into the information-rich and the information-poor, creating a gap that has constantly expanded. Besides, information also segregates people economically. That is, the amount of accessible information determines economic classes. To conceal this fact, as mentioned earlier, the plausible slogan "information overflow" prevails. But we should not forget that, behind this increasingly meaningless "information overflow," people (including artists) feel perplexed, unable to handle overwhelming information. Floating in the ocean of information, they cannot find any point to anchor their authentic lives. While the information realm is increasingly growing meaningless and worthless, we see the emergence of a new information class that monopolizes information to maintain its power and, in contrast, pathetic people (artists included) who lose their identities in endless tides of information. This ambivalent phenomenon revolving around information has given serious and undeniable influence to the contemporary art that deals with information directly or indirectly. As an example of responses to this situation, one can easily think of attempts to exclude information as far as possible by using physical materials and avoiding signs and data. Otherwise, in contrast, artists may actively engage with omnipresence of information instead of being just swallowed in it, trying to reconcile their art with the information-laden reality through effective control and manipulation.

In Japan it seems we have no room between these two extremes. However, no matter how one tries to make their work purely materialistic, it is undeniable this information society soaks into everywhere and allows nothing to escape from its influence. Thus, translation into information is indispensable for any type of expressions to be understood (be reminded that recent works of art are often accompanied by explanatory notes). Still, we can question whether or not we have any alternatives without fully refusing information or being subordinated to it. Now let's analyze the work of an artist, who's practice can be considered as an exception. The name of the artist is Mario A. His 2013 work "When wrong attitudes become radioactive rice"(p.32) consists of several elements. From top to bottom we find a canvas wrapped around an aged wood panel, a photograph of two persons, a canvas covered on a pole sticking out of the wall, a Russian-made Geiger counter on a stand, and a rice bag on the floor. Placed together in relation to one another, these otherwise-ordinary elements=parts signify something tense and urgent.

To begin with, let's look into the photograph. Two persons stand in the foreground against a building, on which one can find neon-lighted numbers and letters - "GIAPPONE 9478.57km". [1]

Here we see a set of sign and data that make up a piece of information, which, if treated as a message to be decoded, means "9478.57km to Japan". The building, or more specifically, the location 9478.57km away from the Fukushima Daiichi nuclear power plants in Japan, is the Japan Pavilion at La Biennale di Venezia in Italy. Additionally, on the white T-shirt of a seemingly Japanese man is an English sentence that reads "ASIANS MUST EAT RICE". It is obvious that this photograph refers to the Great East Japan earthquake on 3/11, 2011, and to the nuclear accidents that followed in Fukushima in particular.

Seen in the context described earlier, we find that this body of work by Mario A also relies on the common use of information in some aspects. Thus, there appears to be little evidence that it differs from other typical artistic practices in regards to information society. However, I didn't want to say that such exceptional artists never make use of information. The focal point is how their strategies evade traps and pitfalls embedded in an environment that is surrounded by an endless flow of information.

This work accepts an orthodox use of information while it instantly sets out for its object (Fukushima). Also, other elements in the work are chosen and deployed so carefully that they all enhance this intention. The wooden board and pole, covered with canvases as a metaphor of art, and the rice in the rice bag were taken from the Fukushima region. The Geiger counter is placed with its manual and package to measure these possibly radioactive materials.

All the descriptions above are found in the information directly printed on the work or captions placed next to it. This work neither excludes information forcefully nor, inversely, relies on it entirely to the point of drowning in the dark ocean of information. Rather, with his excellent sense of balance and calm observation to choose proper pieces of information, the artist seems so clued up as to avoid being enclosed by overwhelming information, and knows the right way to his destination (i.e., the severe nuclear accidents). There are no universal standards to measure such sensitivity and judgement. Artists must stay flexible to contingent situations so that they may find a way out through thick layers of information and let their audience face the proper subject, as Mario A demonstrates masterfully in this work.

Let's shift the attention to the new works of paintings by Mario A. The reason why he has chosen painting as a method of expression now is because he probably started his career as a painter. However, above that, I guess another important motivation for him could be his interest in the predicament of painting, in which contemporary painting is unknowingly trapped. Despite "the death of painting" declared decades ago, this genre not only outlives its proclaimed disappearance but also keeps flourishing especially in the art market. Confronting this situation, Mario A clashes, in a straight forward attitude, with "the end of painting" context by refusing to inform us of his intentions.

Simultaneously, regardless of such urgency facing the art world, he also jumps over the boundaries of painting and art in general in order to make his interventions within reality. Let's see how.

The death of painting was already declared in the past. Back in the 1980s, dying modernism witnessed many people discussing the end of painting. However, even 35 years after that, painting is apparently enjoying the height of its prosperity, and seems unlikely to disappear. Nowadays only a few works can be called as excellent. Or shouldn't I say, we hardly find one? This impoverishment is strongly correlated to a suspicion that painting is really ending today. If the end is finally coming, it's no surprise that there are few strong paintings. With its ending right around the corner, painting can become interesting only when it inscribes awareness of its nearing demise or, whatever comes next, terminates its prolonged life. What brings an end to painting today? Hypotheses on this question will be verified by proving the end of postmodernity, because the end of painting and postmodernism should coincide. This also leads to an expectation that painting may revive in the age following the postmodern.

Let me demonstrate how the postmodern comes to an end. For the sake of clarity, suppose "simulacra" is the principle of postmodernity. If you are not satisfied with this simplified definition, you can also be reminded that the principle of modernity was "materiality". Such simple fundamentals drive history while they produce far more complex outcomes and phenomena.

Incidentally, Jean Baudrillard defined "simulacra" as "a copy without a model", whose representative example he provided by the "product". However, strictly speaking, the product is not a "simulacrum" but a "copy" because it is actually based on a model or a blueprint as the referent. This reveals how postmodernity was conceived and established upon a fundamentally erroneous idea, but in the course of time, such pseudo-simulacra went through a purification process by distilling off impurities (leftovers of models). Its main battle field could at least be found in art, especially painting.

Needless to say, Gerhard Richter is the pioneer of this historical movement since its creation in the 1960s. It is not an exaggeration to state that the trajectory of his painting can be seen as his lifework to explore simulacra (in my terminology: "image without concrete objects") through both realistic and abstract images on the tableau.

Many painters followed Richter, consciously or unconsciously, and tried to incorporate his attempts into their own works in various trial-and-error endeavors, leaving diverse achievements and failures to this day. And now, postmodern painting has reached its final destination, clearly in sight.

As postmodern paradigms have been exhausted, the goal is emerging from the disappearance of barriers that had hindered its progress. There were already two symptoms to suggest this exhaustion taking place. One is that art used up the source of citations to generate simulacra. The history of painting provided references for painting. However, this recycling became no longer possible when the resources ran out. Although one can still reuse something already used (recycling of recycling), such a simple use of the recycled cannot escape from precedents, therefore resulting in a copy but not a simulacrum. This is the only unacceptable violation of postmodern games and their rule of anything goes.

The other symptom is that postmodern painting consumed nearly all of the repertories used to generate simulacra, by deforming or combining cited elements from the past. Although possibilities remain, we will reach the limit sooner or later, at which point simulacra will disappear while everything will be a copy of something in the past. If history comes to an end at the same time as postmodernity ceases, the moment will mark the beginning of a world of post-history. But, if the scenario is not really happening, by good fortune, people in the next generation would be wise enough to start constructing a new history that is neither modern nor postmodern…

Now, let's give a short summary on the paintings of Mario A. It is important to acknowledge his keen consciousness of the death of painting, as mentioned above, and his guts in engaging in such kind of practice. The end of postmodernity can be attested by exhausting its constituents and confining its methods. The day when the archive of quotable elements bottoms out, so will simulacra paintings, which depended on those elements, evaporate into the air. In full knowledge of this reality, Mario A is taking a total affirmative attitude to accept these [art] histories from the past. On the practical side of his creativity, he can do whatever he wishes, just as in the age of anything-goes postmodernity. However, his practice differs decisively from postmodern conditions in that he understands the present reality is not unavoidably similar to something else (this is the nature of postmodernity) but exactly identical to it. Therefore, as seen in his "When wrong attitudes become radioactive rice", he can freely cross over any form and method (no forms any more, hence no contents either) and directly intervene with his target. His criticism is an arrow hitting the targeted reality ahead while penetrating expressions stuck in tautologies. Evading all kinds of obstacles in information society, the magic of Mario A makes its way into the very core of social issues found in his keen critical eye.

1—— This neon sign is part of a work of Koki Tanaka, exhibited at the Japan Pavilion of the 55th Venice Biennale in 2013.

作品リスト｜List of Works

p.14 「Japan = Atom（ガイガー）」2011年、65.2×100cm、キャンバスに油彩
p.15 「Japan = Atom（フクシマ）」2011年、65.2×100cm、キャンバスに油彩
p.16 「ホットスポット」2011年、80.3×100cm、キャンバスに油彩
p.20 「日本の海（I）」2012年、130.3×162cm、キャンバスに油彩
p.21 「日本の海（II）」2012年、130.3×162cm、キャンバスに油彩
p.22 「湾岸の家（I）」2012年、97×162cm、キャンバスに油彩
p.24 「湾岸の家（II）」2012年、97×162cm、キャンバスに油彩
p.25 「湾岸の家（未来）」2012年、97×162cm、キャンバスに油彩
p.26 「富士山（I）」2012年、65.2×100cm、キャンバスに油彩
p.27 「富士山（大）」2012年、130.3×162cm、キャンバスに油彩
p.30 「Cool Japan」（書、prototype A）2013年、45.5×53cm、キャンバスに油彩
p.32 「When wrong attitudes become radioactive rice」2013年、ミクストメディア
p.38 「Caroline in Hiroshima」(Cool Japan) 2014年、45.5×53cm、キャンバスに油彩
p.40 「イクメン」(Cool Japan) 2014年、45.5×53cm、キャンバスに油彩
p.41 「The situation is under control」(Cool Japan) 2014年、45.5×53cm、キャンバスに油彩
p.42 「脱亜論」(Cool Japan) 2014年、45.5×53cm、キャンバスに油彩
p.43 「Ich liebe die japanische Kultur」(Cool Japan) 2014年、45.5×53cm、キャンバスに油彩
p.48 「心」(Cool Japan) 2015年、45.5×53cm、キャンバスに油彩
p.49 「when art is over」(Cool Japan) 2015年、45.5×53cm、キャンバスに油彩
p.50 「Beautiful Japan」(Cool Japan) 2015年、45.5×53cm、キャンバスに油彩
　　 「We ♡ Okinawa」(Cool Japan) 2015年、45.5×53cm、キャンバスに油彩
　　 「Love Me Tender」(Cool Japan) 2015年、45.5×53cm、キャンバスに油彩
p.51 「ricardian equivalence」(Cool Japan) 2015年、45.5×53cm、キャンバスに油彩
p.52 「Cool 九」(Cool Japan) 2015年、45.5×53cm、キャンバスに油彩
p.56 「そうだ」(オレンジ) 2016年、80.3×100cm、キャンバスに油彩
p.57 「そうだ」(レモン) 2016年、80.3×100cm、キャンバスに油彩
p.58 「H32」(Cool Japan) 2016年、45.5×53cm、キャンバスに油彩
p.59 「美・サイレント」(Cool Japan) 2016年、45.5×53cm、キャンバスに油彩
　　 「comme des garçons」(Cool Japan) 2016年、45.5×53cm、キャンバスに油彩
p.60 「おもてなし」(Cool Japan) 2016年、45.5×53cm、キャンバスに油彩
p.61 「Rauschenberg」(Cool Japan) 2016年、45.5×53cm、キャンバスに油彩
p.62 「東京への風（ヒロシマ・ナガサキ・フクシマ）」2016年、97×194cm、キャンバスに油彩
p.66 「原子力明るい未来のエネルギー」（未完）2016年、91×116.7cm、キャンバスに油彩
p.68 「2012年8月17日、国会前「ATOMKRAFT? NEIN DANKE」（原子力？おことわり）」（未完）
　　 2016年、130.3×194cm、キャンバスに油彩
p.72 「Gogh, Kiyoshiro & Me (Summertime Blues -Tokyo 2020)」
　　 2016年、200×103cm、キャンバスに油彩

本書未掲載
「炉心溶融」（未完）2016年、260.6×388cm、キャンバスに油彩

p.14	*Japan = Atom (Gaiga)* (Geiger) 2011, 65.2×100 cm, oil on canvas
p.15	*Japan = Atom (Fukushima)* (Fukushima) 2011, 65.2×100 cm, oil on canvas
p.16	*Hottosupotto* (Hotspot) 2011, 80.3×100 cm, oil on canvas
p.20	*Nihon no umi (I)* (Japanese Sea) 2012, 130.3×162 cm, oil on canvas
p.21	*Nihon no umi (II)* (Japanese Sea) 2012, 130.3×162 cm, oil on canvas
p.22	*Wangan no ie (I)* (Coastal House) 2012, 97×162 cm, oil on canvas
p.24	*Wangan no ie (II)* (Coastal House) 2012, 97×162 cm, oil on canvas
p.25	*Wangan no ie (Mirai)* (Coastal House / Future) 2012, 97×162 cm, oil on canvas
p.26	*Fujisan (I)* (Mount Fuji) 2012, 65.2×100 cm, oil on canvas
p.27	*Fujisan (Dai)* (Mount Fuji / Big) 2012, 130.3×162 cm, oil on canvas
p.30	*Cool Japan* (Sho, Calligraphy, prototype A) 2013, 45.5×53 cm, oil on canvas
p.32	*When wrong attitudes become radioactive rice* 2013, mixed media
p.38	*Caroline in Hiroshima* (Cool Japan) 2014, 45.5×53 cm, oil on canvas
p.40	*Ikumen* (Cool Japan / Child-rearing Men) 2014, 45.5×53 cm, oil on canvas
p.41	*The situation is under control* (Cool Japan) 2014, 45.5×53 cm, oil on canvas
p.42	*Datsu-a-ron* (Cool Japan / De-Asianization) 2014, 45.5×53 cm, oil on canvas
p.43	*Ich liebe die japanische Kultur* (Cool Japan / I love the Japanese Culture) 2014, 45.5×53 cm, oil on canvas
p.48	*Kokoro* (Cool Japan / Heart) 2015, 45.5×53 cm, oil on canvas
p.49	*when art is over* (Cool Japan) 2015, 45.5×53 cm, oil on canvas
p.50	*Beautiful Japan* (Cool Japan) 2015, 45.5×53 cm, oil on canvas
	We ♡ Okinawa (Cool Japan) 2015, 45.5×53 cm, oil on canvas
	Love Me Tender (Cool Japan) 2015, 45.5×53 cm, oil on canvas
p.51	*ricardian equivalence* (Cool Japan) 2015, 45.5×53 cm, oil on canvas
p.52	*Cool Kyu* (Cool Japan / Cool 9) 2015, 45.5×53 cm, oil on canvas
p.56	*Souda* (Soda / Orange) 2016, 80.3×100 cm, oil on canvas
p.57	*Souda* (Soda / Lemon) 2016, 80.3×100 cm, oil on canvas
p.58	*H32* (Cool Japan) 2016, 45.5×53 cm, oil on canvas
p.59	*Bi sairento* (Cool Japan / Be silent) 2016, 45.5×53 cm, oil on canvas
	comme des garçons (Cool Japan) 2016, 45.5×53 cm, oil on canvas
p.60	*O-mote-nashi* (Cool Japan / Japanese Hospitality) 2016, 45.5×53 cm, oil on canvas
p.61	*Rauschenberg* (Cool Japan) 2016, 45.5×53 cm, oil on canvas
p.62	*Toukyou he no kaze (hiroshima・nagasaki・fukushima)* (The Wind towards Tokyo (Hiroshima – Nagasaki – Fukushima)) 2016, 97×194 cm, oil on canvas
p.66	*Genshiryoku akarui mirai no enerugi* (Nuclear Power, Energy for Bright Future) (work in progress) 2016, 91×116.7 cm, oil on canvas
p.68	*2012/8/17, Kokkai-mae 'ATOMKRAFT? NEIN DANKE' (Genshiryoku? O-kotowari)* (2012.8.17, in front of the Parlament building, "ATOMKRAFT? NEIN DANKE") (work in progress) 2016, 130.3×194 cm, oil on canvas
p.72	*Gogh, Kiyoshiro & Me (Summertime Blues - Tokyo 2020)* 2016, 200×103 cm, oil on canvas

not included in this book
Roshin you-yuu (Meltdown) (work in progress) 2016, 260.6×388 cm, oil on canvas

謝辞 | Acknowledgment

かつてのラフカディオ・ハーンやブルーノ・タウトの実績が、次の世紀に至るまで反響しているように、
この作品集が日本の美術界に大きな波を作るという予感があります。
そして、日本の次世代のアーティストのバイブルとなることも期待しています。
私は、日本に来て、私を勇気付けてくれる素晴らしい方々に恵まれたことに、感謝と喜びを感じています。
この場をお借りして、本書を出版するにあたりお世話になったすべての方々に、敬意を表します。

亜 真里男

I do have the feeling that this monograph will make big waves in the Japanese art world.
It will be echoed into the next century like works of Lafcadio Hearn or Bruno Taut.
May this monograph become like a bible for the coming generation of Japanese artists….
It's my pleasure to openly admit that I have such wonderful, encouraging people in Japan around me.
In this sense I would like to express my gratitude to everyone involved in making this precious book possible.

Mario A

市原研太郎	Kentaro Ichihara
青山秀樹	Hideki Aoyama
私の妻 涼子	My wife Ryoko
細川英一	Eiichi Hosokawa
木村稔将	Toshimasa Kimura
ブルーネ・ピーター	Peter Brune
藤川琢史	Takashi Fujikawa
藤束亮太	Ryota Fujitsuka
吉田杏	Kyo Yoshida
細川亜希子	Akiko Hosokawa
木村ナリ	Nari Kimura
スティーヴン・サラザン	Stephen Sarrazin
田村マサミチ	Masamichi Tamura
奥村雄樹	Yuki Okumura
リンダ・デニス	Linda Dennis

略歴 | Biography

亜 真里男［日本のアーティスト］

1959年バーデン・スイス生まれ。ベルリン美術大学中退後、ベルリン大学修士修了。東京都現代美術館他で作品発表。ミヅマアートギャラリーから青山｜目黒 OFFICE（青山秀樹）へ移動。2016年、青山秀樹の青空耳のディレクションにより活躍中。

2016年5月「アートフェア東京」にて個展。2016年9月青空耳（東京の青山｜目黒スペース）にて個展「The situation is under control」。

最近の主な展覧会：2014年 Esther Woerdehoff「Drive In」Paris/Ljubljana；2013年「If walls could speak」ING Collection、Amsterdam、「SOMANYIMAGES」Sprout curation、東京、2012年「亜 真里男個展」アートフェア東京など。

作品集・書籍：『Prélude à la Japonaise』松浦理英子（文）1996年、『F THE GEISHA』多和田葉子（文）1999年、『カメラの前のモノローグ 埴谷雄高・猪熊弦一郎・武満徹』2000年、『ma poupée japonaise』島田雅彦（文）2001年、『マリオ・A 日本美術家』市原研太郎（解説）2004年、『The World Is Beautiful』2006年、『The situation is under control』市原研太郎（解説）2016年、他多数。

日本で最も人気のある現代美術ブロガー・サイト：http://www.art-it.asia/u/sfztpm/
アーティスト・ウェブサイト：http://marioa.com

Mario A ［Japanese Artist］

Born 1959 in Baden, Switzerland. Discontinued studies at Berlin Art University (former HdK). Obtained Master of Arts at Free University of Berlin. Has worked and lived in Japan since the mid 1980s. Mario A became the first so-called "Japanese" artist with non-Asian heritage in the history of Japanese contemporary art. Widely recognized as the most challenging and provocative artist of his generation in Japan.

His works are part of institutional and private collections in Belgium, France, Germany, Great Britain, Italy, Japan, Mexico, The Netherlands, Spain, South Korea, Switzerland and the U.S.A. Nominated for the 'Paris Photo' art fair jury prize 2006. Exhibitions held in the Museum of Contemporary Art, Tokyo, Academy of the Arts, Berlin, Rietberg Museum, Zürich, Museum of Modern Arts, Amstelveen, all important art fairs.

Moved from Mizuma Art Gallery to Aoyama Meguro Office (Hideki Aoyama). Currently directed exhibitions by Hideki Aoyama through Aozora Mimi: Solo shows at the Art Fair Tokyo (May 2016) and "The situation is under control" (September 2016).

Latest exhibitions: Art Fair Tokyo (Solo Show) 2012, ING Collection "If walls could speak" 2013 (Amsterdam), Sprout curation "SOMANYIMAGES" 2013 (Tokyo), Esther Woerdehoff Tokyo Photo 2013, Esther Woerdehoff "Drive In"(Paris/Ljubljana) 2014 – Represented by AOYAMA MEGURO OFFICE (Tokyo), Esther Woerdehoff Gallery (Paris), Elaine Levy Projects (Bruxelles)

Selected monographs: "F THE GEISHA" (1999, text by Yoko Tawada), "ma poupée japonaise" (2001, text by Masahiko Shimada), "Mario A: Japanese Artist" (2004, critique by Kentaro Ichihara), "The World Is Beautiful" (2006), "The situation is under control" (2016, critique by Kentaro Ichihara)

Japan's most popular contemporary art blogger, website: http://www.art-it.asia/u/sfztpm/
Artist's website: http://marioa.com

The situation is under control

2016年5月25日発行

[著者]
亜 真里男

[解説]
市原研太郎

[デザイン]
木村稔将

[印刷]
株式会社シナノ

[発行人]
細川英一

[発行所]
アートダイバー
〒164-0012
東京都中野区本町1-2-3
tel: 03-5352-1023
fax: 03-5352-1023
e-mail: info@artdiver.moo.jp
http://artdiver.moo.jp

ISBN 978-4-908122-04-0